T0114654

The Vision Is Yet For An Appointed Time

CARRIE HALL

BALBOA.PRESS

A DIVISION OF HAY HOUSE

Balboa Press books may be ordered through booksellers or by contacting:

Balboa Press
A Division of Hay House
1663 Liberty Drive
Bloomington, IN 47403
www.balboapress.com
844-682-1282

Because of the dynamic nature of the Internet, any web addresses or links contained in this book may have changed since publication and may no longer be valid. The views expressed in this work are solely those of the author and do not necessarily reflect the views of the publisher, and the publisher hereby disclaims any responsibility for them.

The author of this book does not dispense medical advice or prescribe the use of any technique as a form of treatment for physical, emotional, or medical problems without the advice of a physician, either directly or indirectly. The intent of the author is only to offer information of a general nature to help you in your quest for emotional and spiritual well-being. In the event you use any of the information in this book for yourself, which is your constitutional right, the author and the publisher assume no responsibility for your actions.

Any people depicted in stock imagery provided by Getty Images are models, and such images are being used for illustrative purposes only. Certain stock imagery © Getty Images.

Scripture quotations marked KJV are from the Holy Bible, King James Version (Authorized Version). First published in 1611. Quoted from the KJV Classic Reference Bible, Copyright © 1983 by The Zondervan Corporation.

Scripture quotations marked NKJV are taken from the New King James Version. Copyright © 1982 by Thomas Nelson, Inc. Used by permission. All rights reserved.

Print information available on the last page.

ISBN: 979-8-7652-2588-2 (sc)
ISBN: 979-8-7652-2589-9 (e)

Balboa Press rev. date: 04/12/2023

CONTENTS

ACKNOWLEDGEMENTS

First to my Lord and Savior Jesus Christ who is the author and finisher of my faith. God's precious Holy Spirit that leads and guides me into all truth. Special acknowledgements to Pastor Lawrence Peoples, First Lady Lady Peoples, and my Going Hard For Christ Church Family. Special acknowledgements to my son Thomas Lee Smith and his beautiful wife Kanisha Smith in Okmulgee Oklahoma, my two beautiful daughters Nakia Barnes, and Vikeetra Smith of Tulsa Oklahoma. My sisters Nadine Young Manhattan New York, Sharon Young and my niece Grace Young in Charlotte North Carolina, Iris Teel my sister in Bridge Port Connecticut, and my sister Alice Robinson in Yanceyville North Carolina. Extra Special acknowledgements to Doctor Tyson McMillan my professor at National American University who is my role model, and one of the most intelligent individuals I know. A big shout out to my granddaughter Viqueetra Kinzer in Grapevine Texas. Special acknowledgments to Shirley Hemphill in Brevard North Carolina a friend for over fifty years, God's not through with you yet girl. Special thanks and acknowledgments to James (Sonny) Sitton in Hendersonville North Carolina who is my brother in the Lord for fifty years, and my faithful prayer partner.

SPECIAL DEDICATION

Special Dedication to my mother Nellie Young, and father William Young, and my aunt Irene Gash, and uncle Jim Gash that raised me, and who are my guardian angels watching over me from the balcony of heaven. Gone but never forgotten.

DEDICATION

This book is dedicated to Doctor Lynn Moore over the PhD program, a professor at National American University who has been such an inspiration to me, empowered me, believed in me, and encouraged me to let the ready writer of my pen flow. Special acknowledgements to Doctor Keith McLaughlin, and Doctor Tyson McMillan who inspired me and brought out the best in me. To my cohort future Doctors in my PhD program special thanks, it has been an incredible journey.

To My Adopted Sisters in my PhD program, I will never forget you. I love you all and thanks for the encouragement. Future Doctor Barbara Flores, Future Doctor Jacqueline Rogers, and Future Doctor Debbie Masten, you girls rock.

Special acknowledgements to my three children Tommy Lee Smith Jr, Vikeetra Smith, and Nakia Barnes for their belief in me as a writer and encouraged me every step of the way. Special heartfelt acknowledgments to my oldest sister Alice Robinson in Yanceyville North Carolina, my sister Nadine Young in Manhattan New York, my sister and best friend Iris Teal in Bridgeport Connecticut, and my sister Sharon Young in Charlotte North Carolina, my niece Grace, and my sister Shirley Hemphill Robinson in Brevard North Carolina who I love with all my heart.

A big shout out to Going Hard For Christ Church family, my Pastors, Lawrence Peoples and First Lady Nichelle Peoples for all the love and kindness that they have shown me, and your dedication to the body of Christ. You make a difference in so many people's lives, I love you both dearly. 'Lifestyle Does Matter,' (Peoples, 2023).

Special Thanks and appreciation to Pastor Dean Heath, and his precious wife Pastor Tasheika, your lifestyle and walk with Christ inspires me. I love you both and thank you for praying for me and being an example of what living a saved life really is.

Last but least a big shout out to James (Sonny) Sitton in Hendersonville North Carolina, my brother in Christ and prayer partner. Love, you brother.

A Big thank you to my cousin Tina Oliver in Columbus Ohio, and Mam Dot, I love you with all my heart.

CHAPTER 1

Vision

Do you have a vision that God has placed on the inside of you? What's your vision? When the Lord revealed the vision, he had for me to accomplish my mind was blown. I immediately turned in my bible to Habakkuk 2:2 KJV reads, and the Lord answered me, and said. Write the vision, and make it plain upon the tables that he may run that readeth it Verse 3 says, the vision is yet for an appointed time, but at the end it shall speak and not lie. Thou it tarry, wait for it; because it will surely come it will not tarry. For your vision to come to pass you must write it down and put it in a place where you can see it every day. You will know when a vision is from God because you can't get it out of your spirit. It's deep down on the inside of you and you are constantly reminded and guided towards it. Without a vision whatever you are pursuing will never come to pass. Back in biblical days God spoke to his prophets through dreams and visions. Vision from the Lord always give direction, and it serves people. I've heard a lot of people refer to it as revelation knowledge. When God gives you a vision it uncovers his plan, purpose, and destiny for your life that he predestined from the foundations of the world. A God given visions purpose is to be a blessing to others, and you take the position of servant. Today in 2022 we don't have a lot of visionary leadership like back in biblical days. A God ordained vision reveals the future, is goal orientated, and has an expected date to be accomplished. Each day the visionary is accomplishing small goals that will help bring his or her vision to pass. Any problems that arise the visionary will correct, revamp, and perfect it. It's one thing to receive a vision. Many people in the world have received God given visions but not a lot of visions come to pass. I've met people in my life that had great visions, but their vision died with them and was buried in the graveyard. It's another thing when you don't understand it or know what to do with what you've received. When the Lord revealed the vision, he had for me to accomplish my mind was blown. I immediately turned in my bible to Habakkuk 2:2 KJV. I have a vision board, I speak to it daily, and I'm working towards accomplishing my God given vision daily. You must believe in yourself and be like a racehorse that has blinders on his eyes in a race. Don't look to the right or to the left. You must overlook the haters, ignore the gossip, and keep your eyes on the prize. One way to test your vision is by the opposition that you have. Opposition is the acid test when it comes to vision. Rest is the acid test when it comes to your faith in God to bring it to pass. The most important element for me is the Holy Spirit who is my senior partner in everything that I attempt to do. He leads and guides me into all truth. I personally couldn't think of a better business partner to have. Never give up on your vision even if it takes years to manifest. When you know it's from God, you will trust him to lead you to the right people, make the right business moves, and go forth in his timing not your own. Say out loud with me, the vision that God gave me will come to pass and help people. I want to motivate you to dream big because we serve a big God. If he said it, he will do it and bring it to pass. So many times, in my life I had preachers speak the same word over me that out of me would flow many books. This was told to me in the nineties. I have always journaled every day of my life. I don't watch TV I read. I want to encourage you today that if God gave you a vision don't let it die. Get up and ask God to help you manifest your vision because many people are crying out to God for help. Who knows, your vision may be the one that will be the answer to their cry. You can do it I have faith in you.

Questions

(1) What is your vision?

(2) Has your vision passed the acid test?

Reflections

CHAPTER 2

Devine Delay Doesn't Mean Defeat

Through all the heart ache and struggles that I endured, the one thing that preserved my faith in God was his word. Just because things didn't manifest when I wanted them to God's promises to me were true to my heart. The one thing that I learned through this was Devine Delay Does Not Mean Defeat. Sometimes God intervenes and shuts doors, as well as opens them. There were many days that I was criticized. Talked about and lied on but I kept my faith in God and what he promised me through his word. I know some of my readers can relate to what I am saying. I'm a witness don't let haters, challenges, setbacks, and people who sabotage hold you back. Say this out loud with me, Devine Delay Doesn't Mean Denial. I remember when I was a child and wanted to be on the cheer leading team. They had try outs and I didn't get picked. I came home crying and my dad was there to comfort me. He looked me in my eyes and said to me delay doesn't mean denial Lenny. My dad nick named me Lenny because I was so skinny growing up. At Hill Street school they had auditions for a leading role in a play. I got the lines, rehearsed them every day and got the leading role of Mama Doll in the play. I couldn't wait to get home to tell mom and dad. Dad reminded me of what he had told me. Rejection means redirection, and divine delay doesn't mean denial. Just because I didn't get on the cheer leading squad, God had another plan, and I was in my element. What are some of the gifts and talents that God have given you? Are they lying dormant because of fear of failure? I challenge you to take a step of faith today and believe in yourself. What's your passion, and why haven't you pursued it? God is waiting for you to get up and try it again if it failed the first time. I stir up the gifts on the inside of you and command that they manifest in Jesus's name. I encourage you and empower you to accomplish every goal that you have. In life we tend to always blame the devil. Sometimes it's not the devil holding us back it's us that hold ourselves back. There is something that you are good at, what is it? Find your passion and you will be well on your way to success. I remember when I told friends and family that I was going to write a book. They encouraged me and waited for me to write it. Ten years passed by, and people started saying she's not going to do anything at all. I believe that the divine delay on my book getting finished was nothing but God. At the time I made the statement that I would write a book, I didn't have a clue that I would return to college, complete a bachelor, a master's, and start my PhD program. At present time writing this book I am in my third year PhD program with a 4.0 GPA. I don't take any credit for my academic achievement; all glory and honor go to God. He is the author and finisher of my faith. God began to deal with my heart, and the ready writer of my pen began to flow. I was mocked, looked down on, and kicked to the side. I never lost my faith in God or his promises to me. I journaled every day from age six to present. Even though my book was delayed I knew within my heart that it was indeed an act of God. Don't let anyone, circumstances or anything keep you from fulfilling destiny. Say out loud with me and believe this with your heart. Devine Delay Does Not Mean Denial. I remember the day when I started writing this book. I said out loud that I can do all things through Christ Jesus who strengthens me. Stay positive, and focused. As an author, I realize that it's important to remind people that it's never too late to pursue your dreams. Writing is my passion, what's your passion. Find your passion and remember your gift will make room for you and bring you before great and mighty men. I hope you got something out of this chapter.

Now Is The Appointed Time For Your Vision To Come To Pass!!

Questions

(1) What are the delays that are holding you back?

(2) Is your delay on launching your vision caused by fear of failure?

Reflections

CHAPTER 3

The Purpose of Pain

The purpose of pain to me is to draw you back to God. It is my personal belief that God will allow your heart to break so that the healing process of your soul begins. In life we as human beings can stray away from God, but pain has a way of bringing us back to God on our knees. Pain cannot be ignored it has to be dealt with. A lot of times we refuse to deal with painful issues that are in our heart but when we belong to God, he has a way of causing good to come out of what was intended to break us. There are so many different types of pain, I don't know what you are going through as you read this book, whether it's the pain of rejection, loneliness, or loss. Let me encourage you today that whatever your painful experiences are God wants to heal you. Pain is the door to the next level.

Psalm: 13 King James Version

1 How long wilt thou forget me, O Lord? forever? how long wilt thou hide thy face from me?

2 How long shall I take counsel in my soul, having sorrow in my heart daily? how long shall mine enemy be exalted over me?

3 Consider and hear me, O Lord my God: lighten mine eyes, lest I sleep the sleep of death.

4 Lest mine enemy say, I have prevailed against him; and those that trouble me rejoice when I am moved.

5 But I have trusted in thy mercy; my heart shall rejoice in thy salvation.

6 I will sing unto the Lord, because he hath dealt bountifully with me.

In these scriptures we can see and feel the agony of David's pain as he cried out to God. Pain has a way of making you fall on your knees and humble yourself in the presence of your creator. In this passage of scripture David is broken, he's truthful and precise in the presence of God. Evidently David had been going through this painful experience for some time, he asked God how long do I have to endure this awful pain? David sounds broken, doesn't he? He has come to a point where he is tired, and now in a position of surrender. David felt forgotten, forsaken, alone, abandoned, and troubled. Have you ever felt like David, that you are all alone and not even God hears your cry? If you have felt this way you are not alone, I have found myself in this place also.

David had to trust in something other than his feelings, and he choose God. When we look at this passage in verse 5, David trusted in God's mercy, and he rejoiced in his salvation. This really ministered to me when I read this passage of scripture. I don't know what you are faced with today, but trust in God's mercy and grace to bring you to the other side of your pain. Through these trying moments let's not forget to offer the sacrifice of praise as we process the pain. God has given us a remedy for our emotional pain in his word.

Psalm 34:18 King James Version

18 The Lord is nigh unto them that are of a broken heart; and saveth such as be of a contrite spirit.

Jeramiah 17:14 King James Version

14 Heal me, Lord, and I will be healed; save me and I will be saved, for you are the one I praise.

Matthew 7:7-8 King James Version

> Ask and it will be given to you seek and you will find,
> knock and the door will be opened to you.

I want you to grasp what God is saying to you in the above scriptures as you read this, let it penetrate through the hurt and pain that you thought was so devastating. There is nothing that we go through in life that God can't heal us. I want you to stop reading, close your eyes and take a minute and ask God to help you process your pain. Pour out your heart to him because the Lord is indeed near to you and will heal your broken heart. The word of God gives us further instruction regarding pain, let's dive in the word, and let it have finality over what we are experiencing.

Psalm 139 King James Version

> 1 O lord, thou hast searched me, and known me.
>
> 2 Thou knowest my down sitting and mine uprising, thou understandest my thought afar off.
>
> 3 Thou compassest my path and my lying down, and art acquainted with all my ways.
>
> 4 For there is not a word in my tongue, but, lo, O Lord, thou knowest it altogether.
>
> 5 Thou hast beset me behind and before and laid thine hand upon me.
>
> 6 Such knowledge is too wonderful for me; it is high, I cannot attain unto it.
>
> 7 Whither shall I go from thy spirit? or whither shall I flee from thy presence?

8 If I ascend up into heaven, thou art there: if I make my bed in hell, behold, thou art there.

9 If I take the wings of the morning, and dwell in the uttermost parts of the sea.

10 Even there shall thy hand lead me, and thy right hand shall hold me.

11 If I say, Surely the darkness shall cover me; even the night shall be light about me.

12 Yea, the darkness hideth not from thee; but the night shineth as the day: the darkness and the light are both alike to thee.

13 For thou hast possessed my reins: thou hast covered me in my mother's womb.

14 I will praise thee; for I am fearfully and wonderfully made: marvelous are thy works; and that my soul knoweth right well.

15 My substance was not hid from thee, when I was made in secret, and curiously wrought in the lowest parts of the earth.

16 Thine eyes did see my substance yet being unperfect; and in thy book all my members were written, which in continuance were fashioned, when as yet there was none of them.

17 How precious also are thy thoughts unto me, O God! how great is the sum of them!

18 If I should count them, they are more in number than the sand: when I awake, I am still with thee.

19 Surely, thou wilt slay the wicked, O God: depart from me therefore, ye bloody men.

20 For they speak against thee wickedly, and thine enemies take thy name in vain.

21 Do not I hate them, O Lord, that hate thee? and am not I grieved with those that rise up against thee?

22 I hate them with perfect hatred: I count them mine enemies.

23 Search me, O God, and know my heart: try me, and know my thoughts:

24 And see if there be any wicked way in me and lead me in the way everlasting.

In life we all have experience at some given time feelings of hurt, rejection, absence of self-worth and hopelessness. I have good news today for you, God is our healer, and he wants to heal you. He is the only one that take a walk backwards into your past and heal all your deep-rooted wounds. God had purpose in mind when he created you, and the good news is his plan, purpose, and destiny will come to pass in your life no matter how wounded you are, Jesus can heal you. When he died on Calvary, he took all your pain when he was nailed to the cross by paying the ultimate price.

Isaiah 53:5 King James Version

5 He was wounded for our transgressions, he was bruised for our iniquities, the chastisement of our peace was upon him, and with his stripes we are healed.

Let's just take another minute and let this soak in. Can you imagine the pain Jesus went through when he hung on the cross, obedient to death, and died for us all. Now I think you are beginning to understand what I meant by the purpose of pain. Our Lord and

Savior has gone through every imaginable pain that we could ever go through. He paid the ultimate sacrifice for our healing, so ask him now to heal you. Symbolically we are going to have a funeral right now and bury a series of different pains. Are you ready to bury bitterness, hurt, disappointment, jealousy, low self-esteem, abuse from the past, emotional trauma, rejection, heart ache, betrayal, abandonment, shame, grief, sorrow, depression, loneliness, isolation, sorrow, sadness, rage, and depression? Once you have symbolically buried these things walk away from the burial ground and don't look back.

The healing process of your pain and suffering has now begun. Embrace your freedom, what does it feel like to leave these negative emotions in the burial ground? Raise your hands towards heaven and give God some glory and honor. Let praise become a part of your daily routine, thanking God for all that he has done in your life now and in the days to come.

Psalms 107: 20 King James Version

> 20 He sent his word, and he healed them, and delivered them from their destruction.

Revelations 21:4 King James Version

> 4 He will wipe away every tear from their eyes, and death shall be no more, neither shall there be mourning, nor crying, nor pain anymore, for the former things have passed away.

Psalms 34:18 King James Version

> 18 The Lord is near to the brokenhearted and saves the crushed in spirit.

Psalms 147:3 King James Version

> He heals the broken hearted and binds up their wounds.

Romans 8:18 King James Version

> For I consider that the sufferings of this present time are not worth comparing with the glory that is to be revealed to us.

Jeramiah 29:11 King James Version

> 11 For I know the thoughts that I think towards you, saith the Lord, thoughts of peace, and not of evil, to give you an expected end.

Everyone who has ever been through pain in life can identify with what I'm talking about. Pain is a part of our spiritual growth. Pain uncovers things that are hidden deep in our heart and not like Christ. Pain has a way of purging things out of our heart so spiritual maturity takes place. Pain doesn't discriminate regarding race or gender. Pain on no occasion feels good, but if you will embrace it and allow it to bring you closer to God it will work its perfect work in you. Pain is an emotional process that breaks you, it causes you to bend your knees and cry out to God. The pressure of pain causes you to realize just how much you need God. God is standing there waiting for you to say God I need you, and I can't deliver myself. I don't know what type of pain you are going through as you read this chapter, but I promise you if you will cry out to God the great healer he will come to your rescue. Look at pain as an invite from our heavenly father asking us for permission to do a walk backwards into our past and do an inner healing. When you make Jesus the Lord of your life whatever you go through you realize that you are not alone. God wants to heal you, but he won't unless you allow him to. James 4:8 tells us in the word of God that if we draw near to God, he will draw near to us. When we give our heavenly father an invitation to come in, he will, but remember he only comes by invitation only.

This To Shall Pass

Questions

(1) Name your pain.

(2) What have you learned from your pain?

Reflections

CHAPTER 4

Embrace The Process

Many have asked what the process is, and what does embracing the process mean? Embracing the process means that you made a conscious decision not to concentrate on the negative or disappointments of your past, and you have made up your mind that you absolutely in your heart refuse to be distracted by what might take place or happen tomorrow. Focusing on one day at a time is what you need to do. One day at a time sweet Jesus is all that I can do. As I embrace the process, Lord lead me and guide me by your Holy Spirit. I'm not perfect but I serve a perfect God that chooses imperfect people like me. My sister, what you are going through there is light at the end of the tunnel. Just hold on, embrace every emotion, tears you shed, hurt you feel, and struggles you have been through. Our God's got us. Going through the process I learned that pain is a teacher, it's a stop sign that God gives us, so we don't move any further. Pain is also a guide that will check you before you go down that same path. Pain is like an alarm that notifies you if you try to repeat history, it will check you if you do. If you listen to that inward witness that's on the inside of us, we will avoid a lot of things. My mama told me when I was a little girl, lessons are repeated until learned. I didn't know the depth of what she was saying to me but believe me I understand now. During the times I didn't learn from the things I went through, life caused me to go through them again. The process is all about learning, growing, evolving, and maturing, Pain is part of the process that causes us to bring about change in our lives. Could the process of going through things that are hurtful and painful sends a powerful message that we have gone into the danger zone. Suffering always bring about change. Suffering opens our eyes and allows us to see just how far we are away from God. I don't know where you are in the process as you read this but hopefully you can identify with what I'm saying. The process is preparing you for God's plan, purpose, and destiny. We were all created by God for purpose. When he created us, he placed us on earth to do something for him. We as human beings are so hardheaded, rebellious, stiff necked, prideful, and self-absorbed that we refuse to pay attention to areas in our life where we need growth. The process will break every area where growth is needed and convince us to change. If you are in the valley of the process, remember what I said embrace it don't ignore it.

A Painful Place To Be

Questions

(1) Things you learned through the process.

(2) Has the process made you better or worse?

Reflections

CHAPTER 5

Don't let Your Haters Keep You From Your Destiny

Let your haters become your motivators. If you don't have haters, you aren't accomplishing anything at all. Haters only hate because they feel jealous and envious of your potential and greatness. When they hate on you, they fill some type of sick elevation that makes them feel better because of their inadequacy's. When you are successful in different areas of your life you are a constant reminder to your haters that they are failures. When you are in the spotlight getting attention, your haters aren't happy about that. They want you to be at the bottom with them. Remember misery loves company. Haters never really realize that they have gifts and talents that God gave them, and they don't use them. Hating on someone takes a lot of energy and effort. To be focused on someone with obsession is like having an idol God in your life. Even Paul in the Bible was confronted with haters. If you keep in mind that haters are controlled by demonic spirits, then you will learn that it's the spirit behind the person that causing them to treat you the way that they do. If the word of God tells us in Philippians 4:13, I can do all things through Christ Jesus who strengthens me, then believe it. There will be people who read this book that have stopped moving towards their dreams and destiny because of haters. I want to empower you today, get up, and ask yourself a question. What is my purpose, what did God put me here on earth to do? Find your passion and you will find your purpose. Focus on one of your gifts and stay with it, and above all don't give up. Perfect the gift that God has given you. Don't let negative people, the devil, or demons from hell stop you from achieving your goals. Say this out loud, I'm not going to let anyone, or anything keep me from utilizing the gifts and talents that God gave me. There have been times that I had to encourage myself in the Lord, motivate myself, talk to myself in the mirror, and refuse to give up. The word of God in Proverbs 18:16 plainly tells us that a man's gifts make's room for him and brings him before great men. What gifts do you have that you haven't tapped into? There are people waiting to meet you, places you must go, and God through the ready writer of my pen is saying get up, I've called you to greatness and success. I don't know about you but I'm embracing all my gifts and talents that my heavenly father gave me. My sister Tina Oliver always tells me, sissy you are gifted like a mac truck. All you need is a few good roots to your tree, someone to be accountable to, and realize in your heart that everyone won't go to the next level with you. People enter your life for a reason, and a season. My mother told me as a child that when a person stands before you remember that only two entities could have sent them, either it is God or the devil, it's up to you to discern who sent them. Greatness is calling you, get up out of that grave Lazareth and pursue you God given dreams and passion. There will be many that read this book that the spirit of God will minister to. As I write this, I feel the anointing all over me. God's not through with you yet, it's not over until God says it's over. I have a question, are you going to continue to be beat down in life by your haters, are you going to stop feeling down and realize that you are a child of the most high God. Created for purpose and destined for greatness. God knew while I was writing this chapter in this book that he would be speaking to many who have got their eyes off God, and on their haters. God is calling you to embrace the gifts and talents that are in you. Now is the time, in this dispensation is he calling you to your rightful place.

Questions

(1) Have you allowed your haters to be motivators?

(2) How have your haters limited you?

Reflections

CHAPTER 6

The Holy Spirit Will Be Your Guide Through The Process

Going through the process can be lonely if you don't have the Holy Spirit to guide you into all truth. The process is a journey that can be painful and overwhelming for all who embark upon its path., Jesus left the Holy Spirit as a comforter so if we as Christians will allow him, he will lead and guide you into all truth.

1. Allow The Spirit Of God To Be Your Guide (Rom. 8:4)
2. Renew Your Mind Through The Word Daily And Allow The Spirit Of God To Be Your Senior Partner In Everything You Do (Rom. 8:5)
3. Allow The Holy Spirit To Crucify The Flesh (Rom. 8:13)
4. Be led by the Spirit Daily (Rom. 8:14)
   The Holy Spirit leads us broadly (always) and more specifically (sometimes). He always leads us
5. Get To Know God Through Your Daily Walk With The Holy Spirit (Rom. 8:15–17)

   1. He is the mediator between God and man once you are born again.
   2. The Holy Spirit prays through us.
   3. He affirms with our spirit that we are accepted by God, and we are God's children.

6. The Spirit Is our confidence in the word (Rom 8:22-25)

Embrace the Holy Spirit Daily

Questions

(1) Are you Holy Ghost filled?

(2) Have you allowed the Holy Ghost to guide you?

Reflections

CHAPTER 7

Our Lifeline Is God's Word

God's word has finality over every situation we encounter life. The word of God says many are the afflictions of the righteous, but God delivers him out of them all (Psalms 34:19 KJV). It amazes me in life that we as human beings can believe everyone and everything but God's word. We believe that when we get on an elevator it will take us to whatever floor, we choose when we press the button. We can apply for a job, have an interview, accept an offer, go to work, and work for two weeks, see no money and believe we will get a check. These examples that I've given is faith and belief in action. God is our creature, and we should believe the integrity of his word, meaning the Bible.

Find a scripture in God's word that lines up with what you are going through. I refer to the confession of God's word as gospel-pills. When you go to the doctor, he gives you medicine and you take it three times a day as prescribed by your doctor. You should be confessing the word of God three times a day also. The word says. A merry heart is like a medicine.

Proverbs 17:22

> A merry heart doeth good like a medicine, but a broken spirit drieth the bones.

> God's word transforms our lives when we meditate in it. The word of God say's to meditate in his word day and night. When we put God's word as a priority in our life, he honors his word and watch over his word to perform it.

Joshua 1:8 King James Version

> This book of the law shall not depart out of thy mouth, but thou shalt meditate therin day and night, that thou mayest observe to do according to all that is written therin, for then thou shalt make thy way prosperous and then thou shalt have good success.

> This passage of scripture refers to God telling his servant Joshua to meditate on his word so that he would be successful, and prosperous. So many people today

Psalms 1:2 King James Version

> But his delight is in the law of the Lord, and on his law, he meditates day and night.

As a child growing in up in the Blue Ridge Mountains in North Carolina, I remember driving to Brevard on Sunday with my parents and saying bible verses and singing Jesus Loves Me. What precious memories I have as a child growing up in church and with godly parents. The bible is clear on how we as parents should raise our children. So often we see children stray away from how their parents raised them. Thank God for the Holy Spirit because he always brings back to my remembrance the integrity, substance, ethical values, and character my parents instilled in me from childhood and the values I have today come from my upbringing.

Search The Scriptures
For It Is There That
You Will Find Every
Answer You Need
To Be Successful!!!!

Questions

(1) Do you apply God's word to your Life?

(2) Turn God's word into a confession daily.

Reflections

CHAPTER 8

Don't Let Your Failures Keep You Stuck In A Rut

Countless people today in the world are stuck in a rut and do not have any knowledge or hope of getting out of the rut that they are stuck in. If you are experiencing feelings of being stuck in a rut with your job, family issues, finances, emotions, relationships, or whatever the rut is. If you find yourself feeling stuck like this, you must do something different by acting. I know that what you are encountering feels hopeless, impossible, and even heartbreaking. Today I offer hope to all my readers, hold on to your faith think and see out of the box. It is time to get up and stop feeling sorry for yourself. I know that you have heard this saying that the definition of insanity is doing the same thing expecting different results. Am I speaking to you through the ready writer of my pen? If this hits home for you it is time to generate a plan of strategies that can help you get out of the rut you are in after you make your list of strategies, hopefully, you will be able to see your options and plan to move forward. I remember when a friend of mine ask me why I was so cheerful when I lost a job. My reply to her was rejection means re-direction, and if God is taking me from something he is taking me to something. I could have got stuck in a rut saying woe is me, but I decided to move forward and see rejection as a positive instead of a negative. How are you viewing rejection today, are you still crying over a situation that happened, and are you stuck in a rut because of it? Remember these words from the word of God. We can do all things through Christ Jesus who strengthens us. My advice to you today is to get up, shake the negativity off you, and move forward. Hopefully, the ready writer of my pen gave you hope today so that you see there is life after the rut you were stuck in, and it's full of blessings and God's favor. I'm listing several things that helped me dig my way out of a rut.

1. Change patterns in your daily routine.
2. Regardless of how you feel and what's going on show up.
3. Identify the variance between confrontation and weariness.
4. Find other ways that you can connect with God.
5. Love, live, and laugh.
6. Cry out to God with a pure heart.

When your inspiration has taken flight remember to focus on what the word says, and not how you feel. God knows everything that we as Christians will ever go through. So, if our heavenly father loves us, and knows all about our troubles, trust him through the process and know he will do what his word assures us that he will do.

When I was a little girl growing up in the south, I often would go fishing with my aunt Elizabeth to Tennessee. When we stood on the riverbank waiting to get a bite on our fishing pole, I found so much peace in knowing God was in nature. As I grew older and went through challenges in my life, I found myself gravitating back to the water where I found endless peace. It reminds me of the 23rd chapter of psalms verses one through six. This always brought me out of any rut I was in. This also was a time of devotion with God. There is no reason you should stay in a rut. Meditate on God's word and find scriptures that line up with what you are going through and believe them by standing on God's word, looking at what the scripture says about the circumstances, and not the circumstances. Victory is surely yours if you follow these simple instructions.

Say This Out Loud
With Me. I Have
God's DNA And
There Is No Failure
In God Or Me!!!!

Questions

(1) What are your failures and name them.

(2) What life events caused you to get stuck in a rut?

Reflections

CHAPTER 9

Defeating Failures So Success Is Achieved

I'll start this chapter off by reminding you that fear is only False Evidence Appearing Real. Fear is a paralyzer and will keep you from accomplishing your goals. There is also another obstacle that you must overcome and that is the fear of failure. I went through this myself, and I'm a witness that the fear of failing did hold me back for so many years. Repeat after me no more fear. God created all of us for greatness and sometimes in life we are our biggest enemy. There is a scripture that I found that I quoted daily, and I will share it with you. God has not given us the spirit of fear but power, love, and a sound mind. I quoted this scripture until it got deep down in my spirit. This scripture helped me overcome fear that held me back for so many years. The Holy Spirit allowed me to see that fear was only an emotion that the devil plagued me with for years. Fear will also cause you to procrastinate, and it will stop you dead in your tracks Thank God I'm free from fear, and able to accomplish my goals. When you realize that you will make mistakes, fail, and at times want to give up you will make it. Never let your mistakes, or failures define you. Learn from your mistakes, move forward, and remember that you are no longer stuck in a rut, and just keep on trying. Another reason I failed repeatedly was because I had my eyes on people instead of God. I was raised with a spirit of excellence on my life. My aunt Irene who I called mom that raised me instilled in me from an early age that I had a voice, the sky wasn't the limit, and whatever I did in life, do it to the best of my ability so I would be proud to write my name on it. She often told me that running away from my fears instead of facing them would cause me to fail. I remember her telling me to run to the roar not from it. I loved her dearly and as a child believed everything, she told me. Mama would say to me, don't be intimidated by obstacles, they were placed in front of me so I could overcome them with my faith in God. I'm saying the same thing to you right now use your faith to remove any obstacle that is before you. They were placed in front of you to cultivate growth and move you forward. I want to remind you that you can do all things through Christ Jesus who strengthens you. When God created us, he didn't have failure on his mind. He created us for purpose. God had a plan, purpose, and destiny for our lives. Fear has stopped so many people from accomplishing their goals and moving into purpose. Are you one of those individuals that have backed away from purpose because of fear? Hopefully the ready writer of my pen as I write this chapter has got your divine attention. No more fear, no more stagnation, no more feeling inadequate, and no more procrastinating. Say with me, fear can't hold be back, fear is no longer defeating me, and I'm breaking free from its hold, and moving forward with God. Just because you got stuck in a rut doesn't mean that you as a person is a failure. Repeat this after me no matter how big the failure, or how long I was stuck in a rut it doesn't make me a failure. Get up, move forward, praise God, embrace the Holy Spirit because it is he, that will lead and guide you into all truth.

Questions

(1) How are you defeating your failures?

(2) How are you achieving success?

Reflections

CHAPTER 10

Having Faith Without Works Is Like A Rocket With No Fuel Going No Where

Paul in the New Testament was a perfect example of a man who had weaknesses but needed God and deepened upon God's grace. He wrote approximately twenty eight percent of the New Testament.

2nd Corinthians 12:9 And he said unto me, my grace is sufficient for thee, for my power is made perfect in weakness. Most gladly will I rather glory in my infirmities, that the power of Christ may rest upon me.

Everything that Paul did or went through he always gave God the glory and honor to his heavenly father. We as human beings should never depend or rely on our own ability to accomplish anything. It is very clear in the scripture how Paul boasted in his weakness but gave all the glory to God. When we hear sermons today in church, we hear preachers say Paul molded the faith and narration of the early church. Take a moment and think about what God's grace means to you. Can you as a Christian say that God's grace is sufficient for you? Let's look at what the scripture has to say about grace.

Ephesians: 2: 8-9
Verse 8

> For by grace, you have been saved through faith, and that not of yourselves; it is the gift of God.

Verse 9

Not of works least anyone should boast.

God's grace saves us when we can't save ourselves. Grace causes God to suppress his wrath against us. When I read this scripture, I began to thank God for Jesus, and his shed blood on calvary for the remission of my sins. Here are some more scriptures on God's grace. Study and embrace and meditate on the integrity of God's word. Let it get deep down in your spirit, apply it to your life daily and see the manifestation of grace in your life.

2 Corinthians 8
Verse 8

And God is able to make all grace abound towards you, that you, always having all sufficiency in all things, may have an abundance for every good work.

Take a moment pause, and really think about what this scripture means to you as a child of God. Meditate on these scriptures that expound on grace.

Hebrews 4:16

Let us approach God's throne of grace with confidence, so that we may receive mercy and find grace to help us in our time of need.

Ephesians 2: 4-5
Verse 4

But because of his great love for us, God, who is rich in mercy, made us alive with Christ

Verse 5

> Even when we were dead in transgressions. It is by grace you have been saved.

1 Peter 5:10

> And the God of all grace, who called you to his eternal glory in Christ, after you have suffered a little while, will himself restore you and make you strong, firm, and steadfast.

Titus 2: 11
Verse 11

> For the grace of God has appeared that offers salvation to all people. It teaches us to say no to ungodliness and worldly passions, and live self-controlled, upright, and godly lives in this present age.

2: Timothy 1:9

> He has saved us and called us to a holy life not because of anything we have done but because of his purpose and grace. This grace was given us in Christ Jesus before the beginning of time.

People in society today in 2022 act according to how they feel and what they truly believe in their heart. If we believe that standing in a puddle of water and touching electricity will kill us, we won't touch it. If you as a born-again Christian filled with the Holy Ghost and power sincerely believe God is who he says he is, and the Bible means exactly what it says, you will obey the written word of God and act accordingly. Let's take a walk back in time when you were a child. When your mom and dad told you something you believed them.

That childlike faith should be practiced by us daily as Christians. Our heavenly father talks to us through his word and wants us to believe what is written in the word. Say this out loud, today I'm going to take God at his word, and if God said it, I believe it, and that settles it.

James 2 14-18
Verse 14

What does it profit, my brethren, if someone says he has faith but does not have works? Can faith save him?

Verse 15

If a brother or sister is naked and destitute of daily food

Verse 16

And one of you says to them, depart in peace, be warmed, and filled, but you do not give them the things which are needed for the body, what does it profit?

Verse 17

Thus, also faith by itself, if it does not have works, is dead.

Verse 18

But someone will say, you have faith, and I have works, show me your faith without works your works, and I will show you my faith by my works.

Let's end this chapter by putting our faith into action. Remember faith without works is dead.

Remember You Can Do
All Things Through
Christ Jesus Who
Strengthens You!!!!

Philippians 4:13 KJV

Questions

(1) What do you have the faith to do but no action?

(2) How has faith without action defeated you?

Reflections

CHAPTER 11

Are You Ready To Empower Yourself To Succeed

I have never in life met or read about anyone that was born into this world self-empowered. Self-assurance is learned. We all due to circumstances that we have gone through we have been paralyzed fears and lack of self-confidence. Starting today began to empower yourself, step by step, with persistence and fortitude. In the beginning it may not be easy but if you will stick with it even through the rough and hard times you can be self-empowered. As Christians we won't always have someone to empower, embrace, and encourage us. You have to want to succeed, empower yourself and put yourself in the position to listen to the Holy Spirit who will lead and guide you into all truth, including success. God has given us the power to take control of your own destiny. If you fail, get up and try it again. Failure is a part of success. If we never fail, then how can we ever succeed. Have faith in yourself, and always be humble, not arrogant. When we are comfortable in our skin, our self-image is intact trusting in God, and believing the integrity of his word you will embrace success. Succeed on feedback from others that you are accountable to. People that you are accountable can point out areas in your life that need change, and by doing this you will be able to make the necessary adjustments to better empower yourself. When people give you, constructive criticism don't take it personally but learn from it and improve yourself. It's time for you to get up and focus on getting results and outcomes. When was the last time you focused on your goals, dreams, aspirations, and desires. There is a scripture that comes to mind Zechariah 4:6 says Not by might, nor by power, but by my Spirit, says the LORD of hosts. This scripture lets us know that the spirit of God when embraced will do his job if we will lean on him. Are you ready to allow the Holy Spirit to lead and guide you into all truth? In Philippians 4:13 the word of God tells us we can do all things through him who strengthens us.

It's Time To Get Up And Succeed

Questions

(1) What have you done to empower yourself today?

(2) Have you invested in the tools needed to help you succeed?

Reflections

CHAPTER 12

Your Passion Will Lead You To Your Purpose

What are you passionate about? I remember when I was a little girl, and my mama gave me a diary with a key, and every book that Laura Ingle Wilder wrote for an accomplishment I achieved in school. I was so happy because reading is another passion of mine as well as writing. I began to journal my innermost thoughts, dreams, emotions, events, and things that made me happy and sad. As a child growing up it was a requirement for me to read one book a month. My parents were determined that I would get an education, be able to read, write, and go to college. I am the first person in my entire family and generations that has accomplished so much academically. God gets all the glory and honor for everything he has ever allowed me to be successful in. Identifying your passion shouldn't be hard because it will be something that you love to do and could do it all day every day. When you identify your passions, ask God how to utilize it and be a blessing to others as well as yourself. There are times that God will give me a creative idea, I will begin to allow the ready writer of my pen to take over, and before I realize it, I've started another book. That's passion my friend, and nothing makes me happier than writing. There are people today young and old that have never tapped into their passion. They look at others and wonder why they are successful, and success never comes their way. I can answer that question, they have found their passion. Every person that God created in this world has special abilities and gifts that God equipped them with when they were conceived. Jeremiah 29:11 in the international version says, for I know the plans I have for you, says the Lord. They are plans good and not for disaster, to give you a future and a hope. It is my belief that the minute you were conceived that God had a plan, purpose, and destiny for you. Sometimes it may not so be obvious in the beginning to you. I promise you, if you will take some time and focus on what makes you the happiest, you will find your passion, and purpose. It took me some time to realize that my passion was writing. It's likely that you won't be able to find your passion either right away. I encourage you to keep trying regardless of how long it takes. Just take a moment and think about being able to have a job that you can't wait to get too every day or starting a business working for yourself. Now I know there may be a few people who read this chapter and say, what if I find my passion and pursue it and fail. My advice to you is to do what I did, keep trying and never give up. The more opportunities you find, the more likely you are to discover maybe more than one passion.

Listed Are Several Ways To Jump Start You In Discovering Your Passion

1. Brainstorm
2. Believe In Yourself
3. Utilize Your Gifts and Talents
4. Be Creative
5. Embrace Your Uniqueness
6. Dream Big
7. Don't Be Distracted

Don't Allow Anything Or Anyone To Keep You From Your Purpose!!!

Pursue Purpose With Everything You've Got!!!!

Questions

(1) What is your passion?

(2) What is it that you enjoy doing more than anything else?

Reflections

CHAPTER 13

God's Unwavering Grace Is Sufficient For You

2 Corinthians 12:9
King James Version

> 9 And he said unto me, my grace is sufficient for thee: for my strength is made perfect in weakness. Most gladly therefore will I rather glory in my infirmities, that the power of Christ may rest upon me.

This is one of my favorite verses in the Bible. This verse indorses and causes me to believe that God's grace covers us when we miss the mark in every area of our lives. If you are honest you will agree with me that you to have missed the mark and needed God's grace. There was only one person on earth that was perfect and that was Jesus Christ. Stop beating yourself up because you made a mistake. Get up ask God for forgiveness and do better. Learn from your mistakes and embrace GRACE. God already knew that we would fail in areas of our lives, that's why he gives us grace. If you read your Bible, the moral, the immoral, and the ugly sins that we commit. Don't you ever think for one second that you won't fall short in areas of your life. God is not looking for perfection in us, just maturity, and growth. When we miss the mark, it teaches us that we must depend on God, and it also shows us just how much we need him. Say out loud with me, Lord, I need you. Constantly I recall that the grace of God is a gift that he has given us as believers. There isn't anything good that you could do to deserve it. You can't purchase God's grace either, so just receive it by faith according to God's word. Everyday God opens my eyes to see the sunlight of another day I thank him for his love, and grace that he has extended towards me. Our heavenly father loves us so much and displays his love to us through his word and through daily life encounters. Just take a moment and think about the benefits that we have as believers. Wow, simply mind blowing how our God loves us even at times when we don't even deserve it. When I think about David in the Old Testament and all the evil he did, yet David was a man after God's own heart. Even at your worst God's grace is sufficient for you. If you have been lied on hurt, disappointed, forsaken, rejected, wronged, left for dead, still God's grace is sufficient for you. Grace like peace is something that money can't buy. The richest man or woman in the world can't buy grace. I'm so thankful as a believer for God's grace, aren't you. When I look back over my life all I can do is lift my hands towards heaven, open my mouth and say thank you Lord for your grace and mercy which I embrace daily.

Questions

(1) What has God's grace done for you?

(2) What is your definition of God's grace?

Reflections

CHAPTER 14

Opps, There It Is In The Word Of God

Regardless of what you are going through in life, there is a scripture for you to stand on in the word of God.

1 Peter 4:12

> Beloved, think it not strange concerning the fiery trail, which is to try you, as though some strange thing happened unto you.

If you think for a minute that you are going to glide through life without going through anything you are wrong. Jesus was our perfect example of being without sin and look what he encountered. If you are sick stand on 1 Peter 2:24 Who his own self bare our sins in his own body on the tree, that we, being dead to sins, should live unto righteousness, by whose stripes ye were healed. Were a verb meaning past tense it happened two thousand years ago on calvary. So, if it happened two thousand years ago on Cavalry why won't you just receive your healing by faith. I already know that someone who is reading this is saying I don't have faith. I'm here to correct you and tell you that you do have faith. Have you ever walked up to an elevator and the door opened and you pushed the number seven button. You pushed it because you had faith that the elevator would take you to the seventh floor. Here is another example that you have faith. Have you ever gone on an interview and got a job, was hired and the employer told you that in two weeks you would get a check? You go to work faithfully believing that you will get what your employer told you. That's faith in action. Here is one more example for you. Have you ever entered a dark room hit a light switch and the lights came on? You clicked the switch because you had faith that the lights would come on. My question to you is, why can't you believe God when he tells you something in his word? We can believe man, light switches, elevators, escalators, planes, trains, cars, people, but can't take God's word that's full of integrity at face value. Well, I don't know about you but if God said it, I believe it and that settles it. Whatever you need base it on a scripture in the word of God. Open your mouth and confess the word. Don't be moved by circumstances but by what the word says about circumstances. I thank God daily for his word because it's true from Genesis to Revelations. You will never know for yourself that the word of God is true unless you read it, believe it, and stand firmly upon it believing that the manifestation of what you are believing for will surely come to pass.

Questions

(1) Have you found a scripture to stand on?

(2) What is the scripture you found that you will apply?

Reflections

CHAPTER 15

Walking In Love Isn't Always Easy

John 13:34 – 35
Verse 34

> A new commandment I give unto you. That ye love one another, as I have loved you, that ye also love one another.

Verse 35

> By this shall all men know that ye are my disciples, if ye love one another.

I'm going to be completely honest with you, this is hard to do on your own without the Holy Spirit. Maybe you are like me any many others who have failed in our love walk, repented, and tried it again. Can I be brutally honest with you? Some people aren't loveable and it's hard to love them especially when someone has wronged you and hurt you deeply. If you are like me, I have got mad, upset, and have asked God in the past why do I have to love this person who literally tried to destroy me? God reminds me that he loved me when I messed up and gave me another chance. He's a loving God his mercies are endless, and his love is unconditional towards us daily. What I do is say out loud that I love that person even if I don't feel like I do. It's a faith statement, and I've seen my confession get down in my heart and I went from being so mad, to praying for the individual. That's a start, and a big accomplish for me and more than likely. Regardless of how I feel the word supersedes how I feel or think. I must stand on the promises of God and believe the word. This is a painful place to be in because your emotions are all over the place. We condemn ourselves most of the time before others do, and that's a good thing because we come to realize that these are issues of the heart. So many times, I have been in the presence of God crying out to him because I felt like this love walk wasn't for me just Jesus. I made up every excuse in the book why I couldn't do it, does this seem familiar to you? Trying to justify wrong in the presence of God is a losing battle. If you will be honest right now and you be truthful with yourself you will say, I did the same thing. The love walk is a faith walk; I truly mean a blind faith walk. The reason why I say this is because I have experienced it firsthand with family, friends, and associates. Our family members know us and push our buttons daily. It's up to us not to respond in a negative way. We have choices and believe me we as Christians don't always make the right ones. God's grace is needed in this situation and help from the Holy Spirit to overcome the emotions we feel when this happens. Walking in love has a way of shifting the atmosphere at home, in the workplace, and with people who aren't loving. Let's all make a commitment to work on our love walk. Say this with me, Holy Spirit I can't walk in love the way God wants me to. I need your help. Jesus said you would lead and guide me into all truth. By doing allowing him to help us it will bring about change in our love walk toward people.

Questions

(1) What's keeping you from walking in love?

(2) Has unforgiveness hindered your love walk?

Reflections

CHAPTER 16

Write The Vision Plainly

Habakkuk 2 1-3
Verse 1

> I will stand upon my watch, and set me upon the tower, and will watch to see what he will say unto me, and what I shall answer when I am reproved.

Verse 2

> And the LORD answered me, and said, Write the vision, and make it plain upon tables, that he may run that readeth it.

Verse 3

> For the vision is yet for an appointed time, but at the end it shall speak, and not lie though it tarry, wait for it; because it will surely come, it will not tarry.

Has God given you a vision for success? This is the acid test to see if your vision is from God. If you can fulfil your vision, it's not from God. On the other hand, if your vision is so large that you can't begin to imagine how to fulfil it, that's a vision from God. A true vision from God will always bring advancement to the kingdom of God and help others. If your vision is God sent, it will give glory to God always. A God given vision will be an answer to others prayer and bring solutions to their problems. Vision is essential for any leader in 2022 because without a vision the people will surely perish quickly. I want you to do something for me. Get a poster from the Dollar Tree and make you a vision board. Write down your vision, short term goals, long term goals, and make sure that they are realistic and attainable. Set a time range when they will be accomplished. Every vision that is from God the future can be seen it. Here is some free advice that won't cost you a dime, never be in a church that doesn't have vision, or don't work for a company that the leader doesn't embrace vision. If you are a business owner, you must have vision and core values. Ethics must incorporate your vision if it's truly from God. My desire is to see everyone who reads this book accomplish the God given vision that God gave them. Hopefully, this chapter of my book will equip every reader including myself to bring the vision that God has placed in our hearts to pass, so God is glorified.

A Vision Prayer

Father in the name of Jesus, Holy Spirit enlighten every reader to embrace and bring the vision that God has placed in their heart to pass. We all have unreleased potential that was place on the inside of us by God. Bring our visions to pass so that we can fulfil your plan, purpose, and destiny for our lives. Father god there are people waiting to meet us. We are an answer to prayer for many who have bowed their knees before you and asking you to send somebody. There is a gift on the inside of us that was meant for humanity to benefit from. With your help father God, we will accomplish everything that you have equipped us to do. You gave us this vision, and gifted us dear God, and we trust you to bring it to pass so the world can see the manifestation in Jesus' name, Amen.

Believe In Your God
Given Vision!!
See Yourself There!!
Don't Let Anything
Hinder You!!

Questions

(1) Have you written your vision down?

(2) Do you speak faith filled words over your vision?

Reflections

CHAPTER 17

Godly Leadership

We have the world's definition of leadership and God's definition of leadership. A spiritual leader will always be interested in displaying God's power in his leadership position. It can also be defined as comprehending where God wants individuals to be and taking the ingenuity by applying God's word, prayer, and the Holy Spirit, that will change people's lives so that they can reach their destination. Great spiritual leaders have vision, accountability, compassion, humility, integrity, substance, values, character, confidence, honesty, creativity, high ethical morals, and empathy just to name a few. We all know some influential spiritual leaders that have made an impact on our lives. I'll name a few that had a major impact on my life. Kenneth E Hagin and Oretha Hagin, Oral and Evelyn Roberts, Marty Papp, Richard and Lindsey Roberts, Clinton and Sarah Utterbach, Creflo, and Taffy Dollar, RC and Lisa Blakes, TD and Serita Jakes, Fred and Betty Price, Kenneth and Gloria Copeland, Clearance and Pricilla McClendon, and Bill and Veronica Winston. I know you are wondering why these leaders made such a life changing impact on my life. Their love walk was what caught my attention, and their integrity in ministry. While we do not have one set definition for leadership, the examples above paint a leader as someone who has a strong strategic vision and goal, knows how to motivate, and mobilize people around that goal and knows when to listen and follow others who bring their own skills and qualities to the table.

Never Follow Any Leader That Doesn't hear From God!!!!

Questions

(1)   Do the leaders in your life have high
       ethical values?

(2)   Do you see integrity in your leader?

Reflections

CHAPTER 18

Unethical Leadership

The world today is filled with unethical leaders who don't embrace high ethical values. There used to be a time in the past when preachers were ethical, but not anymore. We see some of them living like the world and enjoying their wrongdoing. I'm not saying all preachers are like this I said some are. You can't tell them from the world. If you are under an unethical leader weather it's a boss, or preacher you had better remove yourself from that situation. Today in leadership everyone is wanting to make money, get a head, and they don't care who they hurt or destroy to get to the top. Integrity is a thing of the past, and morals have gone out the window. Unethical leaders destroy people and everything they touch become contaminated. When was the last time on your job you stood up for what was right, versus saying it's not my problem if I'm getting paid? Unethical practices in business or the church causes so much pain to innocent people that aren't aware of their wrong doings. Religion now days is so full of games and gimmicks instead of ethical values. How can a preacher preach the word and be unethical? Mammon, meaning the love of money has caused many good men and women to stray away from high ethical values. Some churches have become unethical and embrace practices that aren't ethical at all. So many times, people will start out right but end up wrong. Have you seen leaders and people in high positions like that? I have and it hurts me to the core of my soul. Back in the day the Ojay's wrote a song For The Love Of Money. Well today in 2022 we see the words of the song in full manifestation in the world. Have you ever asked yourself what caused them to turn from being ethical to unethical? I've asked myself that question on numerous occasions and see a lack of moral values in people like that daily lives. We as Christians must always embrace and walk in integrity. Always to the best of our ability pursuing ethical not unethical principles. The older I get the more I see unethical practices in ministries and business. My prayer has been for a very long time that God remove these people from ministries, business, government, and the white house that have unethical practices. What would you do today if you knew something was done wrong and if you told it, you would lose your job? Would you tell it and lose your job, or keep your mouth shut and allow unethical practices to continue to be done? My answer is I would rather lose my job and have a clear conscience by telling the truth and following my own convictions. Everyone reading this chapter in my book should be praying that God will remove people from positions that embrace unethical practices. Being unethical as a leader affects everyone, and everything around them. Embrace your ethical values, and if God is calling you to be a leader be an ethical leader with integrity and high ethical values.

Don't Be An Unethical Leader!!

Questions

(1) Can you identify unethical leadership in your leader?

(2) Can you name some unethical traits in leaders?

Reflections

CHAPTER 19

How To Receive From God The Correct Way

To receive from God, it must be done the correct way according to the word of God and not you're on intellect. During difficult time when my faith was being tried this is what I did, and I received victory. To be successful in this area you can't look at the circumstances, only what the word of God says about the circumstances. The time has come when we as Christians must be doers of the word and not hears only. Practice this daily until you receive the manifestation of what you have prayed and believed God for. It's not Burger King you don't get it your way so empty all your perceptions on how it should be done and allow everything to line up with the integrity of God's word. Keep in mind you have what you say so put a watch on your mouth and don't allow anything negative to depart from your lips.

1. Find a scripture in the word of God that deals with what you are going through.

2. Let that scripture come out of your mouth daily through confession.

3. Begin to call those things that are not as though they were.

4. Don't let anything contrary to the word of God come out of your mouth.

5. Faith, Love, and Patience are partners in receiving from God.

6. Believe that you receive what you asked God for.

7. If you have unforgiveness towards anyone forgive.

8. Continue all the above, and rest in the promises of God.

Psalms 103:20

> Bless the Lord ye his angels, that excel in strength, that
> do his commandments hearkening unto the voice of
> his word.

I don't know if you are aware that angels listen for God's word to be spoken, and they move when they hear the word of God coming out of our mouth. Don't just sit there and allow the devil to win, we have the victory through the spoken word of God. I don't have a clue as to what you are going through as I'm writing this book, but I know that we defeat the devil by speaking the word of God, believing we receive, and praising God for the Victory. Say out loud with me. I have the victory in the name of Jesus. That victory was purchased for me two thousand years ago on Calvary and I receive it by faith.

Now just take a praise break and give God some radicle praise. The type of praise that will send the devil and his demons on the run. Thank you, Lord, that when we open our mouths and speak the word circumstances change.

The Only Way To Receive From God Is The Bible Way!!

Questions

(1) Do you believe what the Bible say's about receiving from God?

(2) What was the last thing you prayed about and received from God?

Reflections

CHAPTER 20

A Word Of Wisdom To The Ladies

I'll start this chapter off by saying if you can't be alone, you aren't ready for marriage. Ladies you must learn to love yourself. Take yourself out to a five-star restaurant, go on vacation, treat yourself, and take yourself out to a movie Fall in love with YOU. Send yourself a dozen of roses and some balloons. I'm going to enlighten you by telling you the truth. Some of the loneliest people in the world that I have met are married people. It is my belief that part of the reason they are lonely is because they had this preconceived idea that marriage was the honeymoon. The truth is marriage is WORK.

Being single is one of the best things that could have happened in my life. In my singleness and being alone I got to know myself. How many of you that are reading my book really know you? Women are looking for a man to define them. Ladies do you understand that you are unique. In other words, be an original and not a copy. There isn't another woman in the world that I would want to be other than myself. Know your worth, embrace yourself, and know your value. There are so many women that have put their self on the sales rack running after a man. Listen to me, wake up and get yourself back in the show case where the valuables are kept. Say this with me, I'm beautiful, unique, fabulous, anointed, intelligent, and in love with my God and me. I empower you in this chapter to be the best you. You are only ready for marriage when you don't need to be married. I believe that this is the acid test to being single.

It's time that we as women learn that marriage isn't the most important thing in life. Let's take this time to work on ourselves and become a better person. Remember ladies what the word of God says in the scripture

Proverbs 18:22

> Whoso findeth a wife, findeth a GOOD THING, and obtaineth favor of the Lord.

I am heart broken when I see women running after a man. Your King will find you when you do it God's way and not your own. Today in society a woman can meet a man and the brother is in the bed with her before the night is over. If you are a woman reading this and going from relationship to relationship, closure starts with your legs. Believe me I didn't studder at all when my advice came out of my mouth. Stop being so easy, where is your self-esteem, and love for yourself. Sex is for marriage and marriage only. We have all made mistakes and thank God that he is a forgiving God. Ladies remember this, dating is for data and data only. I refuse to allow my King to see the fingerprints of another man on me. Say this out loud with me, I'm a Queen and I'm not easy. The only way you as a man can have me is go through my father God. Respect yourself ladies because if you don't know man will. Wait on the Lord, this is your time if you are single to work on you. Shine like that diamond that you are and remember to celebrate you.

Questions

(1) Do you check yourself before you wreck yourself?

(2) Are you a wise woman that embraces and obeys the word of God?

Reflections

CHAPTER 21

Be An Original And Not A Copy

Always be an original and not a copy. God created all of us different and unique. If you will take a deep look inside of yourself, you will clearly see that trusting God given instinct and intuition is a major part of you really knowing yourself. God has placed them both inside of us, as well as given us the Holy Spirit who brings all things to our remembrance. I like being an original because to me it means, you don't run with the crowd, associate with clicks, and copy another individual. Originals always go to the manufacture of them which is God and ask for creative ideas, guidance, and help. Originals depend on God totally to enlighten them and move them in the direction that they need to go in. What makes you stand out from others? Originals are out of the box thinkers, and always see the big picture. They are self-motivated, task orientated, and have a keen sense for organizational skills as well as time management. My motto has always been, why run with turkeys when you can soar with eagles. An eagle can fly above the storm. When I lived in Asheville North Carolina one of my favorite spots was Buzzard Rock. I often sit there and watched the eagles soar through the sky. It always amazed me the length of their wingspan. The eagle always got my attention and God taught me valuable lessons when observing them. You never see an eagle hanging out with chickens or turkeys. Even though they are a part of the bird family they know who they are and stay in their own lane. Ask yourself a serious question. Are you hanging out and running around with chickens and turkeys. Who are you accountable to? Who are the people that are in your inner circle? Only you can answer those questions and know if you are an original or a copy. Develop your own style regardless to what styles are in. I personally have my own style, and love being authentically me. A lot of people like Mercedes Benzes but me, my personal choice of my ideal car would be a 1975 Impala Convertible, pearl white, with white wall tires, ivory leather seats, and an acrylic pearl steering wheel. I set my own trend when it comes to fashion. I love designing jewelry in my spare time and get creative ideas from God all the time. The ideas that I get are originals because I haven't seen a piece of jewelry that I've made in any stores. Being an original came about in my life by cultivating and developing myself. You know when you are an original because you don't care what others think. To be an authentic original, you must be secure, comfortable in your own skin, confident, and never endeavoring to be anyone else but you. When you make a conscience decision to take the time to spend time refining your own technique, tastes, and persona, this adds to you being genuine and an original. People around you will find you to a greater extent fascinating and striking to others. Originals are fearless, and they embrace their originality, Let go of fear and embrace your uniqueness, and most of all know who you are. Originals don't every compete with anyone but themselves. Little girls and boys compete, originals never do. Ask yourself today this question. Am I an original or just a copy of another person you admired? In selecting the right direction for yourself, make sure that you never allow what someone else thinks, or their opinions get you off course. Never ever second guess yourself, always embrace what you believe in, especially when it lines up with your ethical values. If you are an original, the one thing you will know for sure is the capacity of your exceptional abilities and gifts that your heavenly father has given you.

Questions

(1) Are you an original?

(2) Do you allow people's opinions to stop you?

Reflections

CHAPTER 22

Realizing Your Self Worth

This chapter embraces self-worth, something that few women have that I encounter. I have a question, why do allow people to define who you are? I've met people with such low esteem that have went through challenging times, and because of what happened or what somebody said about them. When you allow others to define your life, accomplishments, future, success, goals, and what you can visualize you are destined for failure. You got to know your value, and self-worth, especially what you bring to the table. When you know your self-worth, you won't down grade and accept just anything or anyone that comes along. God placed everything inside of you to be successful. The problem is some people never tap into their potential. Fear paralyzes them, what people say stops them, and ultimately, they find themselves stagnated by how someone else perceived them. You, yes you are writing the script of your own happiness daily, and you are the one that is responsible for your own success or failure. Self-worth consists of boundaries, respect for yourself, realizing what you deserve, never settling for less than what you deserve, being true to your own set of ethics and values. When you realize your self-worth certain things will begin to manifest through you. This manifestation will include, self-love, not fearing being alone, removing toxic people from your inner circle, achieving goals, becoming the very best version of yourself, ignoring what others say about you, evolving, can't be a part of your vocabulary, realizing that your time is precious, and everyone doesn't deserve some of it. Rapidly, you will comprehend that it's better to be alone, content, have peace, happy than to be with someone that pushes your buttons taking you on scary emotional roller coaster rides. Does this sound familiar to you? Let's be honest and transparent, every one of us has gone through this. As for me, I learned by lessons that I needed to learn, and refuse to allow anyone to reduce me, and go back to Egypt. Your self-worth will cause you to qualify people before you allow them to enter your life. Because my self-worth is intact, I will only allow a man in my life that reciprocates all the above that was written. Self-worth causes you to encourage yourself when there isn't anyone there to encourage you. You will confess over yourself what you want to see manifest in your life. Say this out loud with me, I'm in the process of becoming the best version of me and refusing with every fiber of my being to be an original and not a copy. When you have self-worth you will leap over obstacles, accomplish goals, and be happy by yourself. We can't do anything about the past, but we can do something about our future. By now you should be motivated, challenged, empowered, determined, excited, and ready to work on loving you more than you ever have in your life. Father God, please allow everyone that read this chapter come to realize that self-worth is extremely important in the journey of life. I thank you Lord for people you have predestined to read my book. Bless everyone who turns the pages of this book. Let the presence of God rest upon every word that I write. I won't forget to give you the glory and honor in Jesus's name. Now Holy Spirit perfect my readers in every area of their life that needs to be perfected. In the matchless name of Jesus I pray, Amen. It is my heart's desire that this chapter in my book ministered to you. Be the person who makes up their mind and say, I will never allow anything or anyone to mess with my self-worth anymore. I'm blessed, and on my way to success, never looking back at past mistakes but embracing opportunities coming my way each day. Change your mind set by recognizing that God is the pilot, and you are the messenger.